Catechist's
Guide

How to Teach Scripture

How to Teach Scripture

Biagio Mazza

Paulist Press
New York/Mahwah, NJ

Cover and book design by Lynn Else

Library of Congress Cataloging-in-Publication Data

Mazza, Biagio.
    How to teach Scripture / Biagio Mazza.
        p. cm. — (Paulist catechetical guide series)
    ISBN 978-0-8091-4630-7 (alk. paper)
    1. Bible—Study and teaching—Catholic Church. I. Title.
    BS600.3.M324 2010
    220.6'1—dc22

                                                             2009037245

Published by Paulist Press
997 Macarthur Boulevard
Mahwah, New Jersey 07430

www.paulistpress.com

Printed and bound in the
United States of America

Contents

A Word of Welcome to All

Welcome to all catechists who are making time to pick up this book and read. Welcome to an adventure in learning. Most especially, welcome to an adventure in growing and deepening your love relationship with God's Word.

The Bible is the medium through which God speaks to us with words of joy, challenge, compassion, and love. Our love relationship with God is fine-tuned through our desire and willingness to enter into communication with God in and through the Bible.

This book is an entry into our love relationship with God by means of God's Word. It is an attempt to explore the various facets of that relationship. We are made up of head, heart, and feet. The questions on the different aspects of the Bible and its use in our community celebrations and our learning environments are an attempt to feed our head and heart. Once we have nourished our head and heart, our feet will lead us into the path of life.

You are a source of light to all those you come into contact with. May this book be a source of life and light to you in your own love relationship with God and with all those whom God directs your way.

As you undertake this adventure, you will be exposed to what the Bible is and how to read, interpret, and understand it.

1
What Is the Bible?

The Bible is God's Word in human words. Catholics believe the Bible to be the very Word of God, communicated to us in and through the writings of humans. These books are collections of the faith reflections of various communities at different times in humanity's journey with God.

We believe that God communicates with us in a multitude of ways. We do know that God does not usually communicate with us in the same way we communicate with each other. Rather, God communicates with us in and through the everyday experiences of our lives. It is within those life experiences that the roots of the Bible are found.

The Bible consists of the human faith experiences and reflections of people who have tried to sort out how God was present in their lives. That is the human side of this book. Different faith communities, at different times, with different questions and concerns, reflected on God and how God spoke to them in their own unique contexts. Over the centuries, they wrote those reflections down so that others would learn and gain insights from these interactions with God.

Where is God in this process? God is the divine instigator of this faith journey, as well as the one who revealed what needed to be said, inspiring the minds and hearts of those who believe. We believe that God speaks to us in and through the faith reflections of those who have gone before us "marked with the sign of faith," as noted in one of our Eucharistic Prayers. God insures that what is being shared contains the truth that God wants communicated. But that communication occurs in and through the human reality of particular words, thoughts processes, time, space, and events.

Ultimately, the Bible is truly God's Word coming to us in and through all of life's experiences and the resulting faith reflection on those experiences. We continue to read the Bible because we believe that through those faith reflections of long ago, God continues to speak to us today, guiding and directing us through the message of this written text. The Bible continues to be for us a living book, communicating God's Word for our time.

1. Reflect on how God speaks to you today in and through your lived experience.
2. What do you understand God saying to you as you reflect on your unique situation and context in life?

WHAT IS BIBLICAL FUNDAMENTALISM AND HOW DO WE, AS CATHOLICS, RESPOND TO SUCH A BIBLICAL MINDSET?

In 1993, the Pontifical Biblical Commission issued a document titled "The Interpretation of the Bible in the Church." This document defines fundamentalism as biblical interpretation that "starts from the principle that the Bible, being the word of God, inspired and free from error, should be read and interpreted literally in all its details...which excludes every effort at understanding the Bible that takes account of its historical origins and development."

Biblical fundamentalism is a mindset cutting across all religious denominations. Fundamentalists read and interpret the Bible literally, placing exclusive emphasis on the divine dimension of the Bible. All the human dimensions of Scripture, such as literary styles, historical context, origins, and development, along with various other "human" realities, are ignored, downplayed, or denied.

This perspective has the biblical books being dictated by God to the human authors by means of various divine beings, such as angels. In this context, the word *inspiration* is used to claim that God took over the spirit of the authors and told them exactly what to write and how. Humans really had nothing to do with the text of Scripture since they got it word for word directly from God.

Therefore, the Bible is GOD's Word, meaning that there are no factual or narrative errors whatsoever in Scripture, and that the way it is written is exactly the way things happened. The Bible is understood to be the actual, factual account of the events recorded, being accurate historically, factually, and in all other ways. Since God is the author of the Bible, the Bible is inerrant, that is, it contains no errors whatsoever. Apparent errors or contradictions are text that has not been rightly interpreted or understood.

Fundamentalists believe that by simply picking up the Bible and reading the text, one will easily understand the meaning of the text, along with what God is trying to say through that text, and how to apply that text to one's life. Bible reading and its corresponding interpretation are just not that simple.

1. How would your respond to someone who had a different approach to the reading and interpreting of scripture?

WHAT DO THE WORDS *REVELATION, INSPIRATION,* AND *CANON* MEAN WHEN THEY ARE APPLIED TO THE BIBLE?

The word *canon* has its source in a Greek word meaning "ruler or measuring stick." When applied to the books of the Bible, canon refers to the list of books we now have enshrined in the Bible along with their sequence. This canon is considered to be the measuring stick against which all who accept the Bible as the Word of God are to measure their lives and actions. Once a text is accepted as canonical by the community, there can be no further changes made to the text. Understanding or interpretation of the text may change, due to different information or circumstances which arise, but the text is firmly set, not to be changed.

What leads a community to select some texts as canonical and reject others? The Christian community used several criteria for this selection. The text had to be associated with an apostolic person in some fashion, assuring the authenticity of its witness. The text had to have been in wide use among various Christian communities over a long period of time. The text was considered by all who experienced it as an orthodox and authentic witness to the reality of Jesus. If a text met these criteria, then it was accepted as canonical. There was much argument and disagreement over the final list, but by 400 AD, a definite list of books had been accepted, forming the New Testament as we have it today.

If a text was considered canonical, it meant that it was inspired by God. To be inspired meant that God was present throughout the whole process of the text's development, insuring the truth and validity of what God wanted to communicate for our salvation. God did not dictate the text to the authors, but guided them in a nonintrusive fashion to use their individual creativity and intelligence. God worked through each one's creative processes to insure that God's Word and truth would be communicated. The authors used their knowledge of God and their communities to reflect on the faith events that had taken place in their midst and to creatively fashion that story for their communities' needs and concerns. God assured that in that creative process, divine truth was communicated.

Revelation refers to God, who from the very beginning initiated the process of moving out of self into relationship with all of creation. This invitation and call by God we call *revelation*. God's initial step invited us to enter into the divine dance with God, allowing each of us to know more and more about God. This "more and more" we call revelation. Through God's revelation of self, we come to learn who God is, who we are, why God created us, and what God intends for us and asks of us.

1. List some of the things that God has revealed to you in and through life's experience, in and through God's inspired Word, and in and through others' words, insight, and modeling.

HOW DO YOU LOCATE A PASSAGE IN THE BIBLE?

The following points explain how a Bible reference works. In any biblical reference, the following elements are usually present. It would be good to use a Bible to follow along with these points:

1. Each book of the Bible has a separate name. The full name of the book or its abbreviated form is the first information that one encounters in a biblical reference.
   - Matthew means the Gospel of Matthew. Isaiah means the Book of Isaiah.

- Matt also means the Gospel of Matthew. Isa also means the Book of Isaiah.
2. If there is a number in front of the title of the biblical book, that means there is more than one book called by the same name:
   - 1 John means that there is more than one book named John.
   - 2 Kings means that there is more than one book named Kings.
3. The full or abbreviated name of the book may be followed by numbers. The first number means the whole chapter of a particular biblical book. If the first number is followed by a colon (:), the second number means a particular verse within that chapter is being referred to.
   - Romans 3 means Paul's Letter to the Romans, all of chapter 3.
   - Romans 3:15 means Paul's Letter to the Romans, chapter 3, verse 15.
4. A hyphen (–) between numbers means that several chapters or verses are being referred to. If there is no colon, the numbers mean entire chapters.
   - Romans 3–7 means Paul's Letter to the Romans, all of chapter 3 through all of chapter 7.

If there is a colon, the numbers after the colon mean several verses, or two or more chapters and verses.
   - Romans 3:4–9 means Paul's Letter to the Romans, chapter 3, verses 4 to 9, including verse 9.

- Romans 3:7–4:12 means Paul's Letter to the Romans, chapter 3, verse 7, through chapter 4, verse 12, including verse 12.

5. A semicolon (;) between numbers means different passages within the same book, or different passages within several books.
   - Romans 5; 7 means Paul's Letter to the Romans, all of chapter 5 and all of chapter 7.
   - Romans 5:2–7; 1 Peter 1:13 means Paul's Letter to the Romans, chapter 5, verses 2 to 7, *as well as* the First Letter of Peter, chapter 1, verse 13.

6. A comma (,) between numbers means separate but not continuous verses from the same chapter.
   - Romans 11:1, 4, 9, 13 means Paul's Letter to the Romans, chapter 11, verses 1, 4, 9, and 13.

7. A letter added to a verse number means a verse that has been divided because of its length, but the biblical quotation does not refer to the other parts.
   - Romans 4:2–3a means Paul's Letter to the Romans, chapter 4, verse 2 through only the first part of verse 3.

8. An *ff* following a verse number means an indeterminate number of verses following the numbered verse, usually until the topic or theme changes.
   - Romans 9:8ff refers to Paul's Letter to the Romans, chapter 9, verse 8, along with an indeterminate number of verses after verse 8, usually until the topic or theme of the writing changes.

WHAT IS THE BEST WAY TO READ AND INTERPRET A BIBLICAL TEXT?

To understand and interpret a biblical text properly, one needs to be attuned to the mind and heart of the community that put the text together. It is important to examine the historical context, along with the culture and mindset of that community. The sources used, as well as the text's literary style, also need to be examined. All this will ultimately help get to the message that God wanted to express through this faith community.

> In order to discover *the sacred authors' intention*, the reader must take into account the conditions of their time and culture, the literary genres in use at that time, and the modes of feeling, speaking, and narrating then current. (*Catechism of the Catholic Church* #110)

Of course, that message is also the truth that God desired to communicate at that time and context to help that community in its faith journey. We continue to read those texts today because we believe they continue to help us in our faith journey as well, especially in our desire to know our God and what God expects of us.

A preparatory document put together by the Vatican Pontifical Biblical Commission that was eventually incorporated into the Vatican II Constitution on Divine Revelation, *Dei Verbum*, might be of help. Titled "On the

Historicity of the Gospels," the commission makes the following statements regarding the composition of the biblical books, with primary focus on the Gospels:

> The sacred authors, each using an approach suited to his specific purpose, recorded the primitive teaching in the four Gospels for the benefit of the churches.
>
> Of the many elements at hand they reported some, summarized others, and developed still others in accordance with the needs of the various churches. They used every possible means to ensure that their readers would come to know the validity of the things they had been taught.
>
> From the material available to them, the Evangelists selected those items most suited to their specific purpose and to the condition of a particular audience. And they narrated these events in the manner most suited to satisfy their purpose and their audience's condition.

One can see the human process involved. At the same time, the truth that God wanted communicated was assured through divine inspiration. Hence, the Bible is a totally human product that is at the same time totally divine, inspired and directed by God every step of the way.

WHEN TRYING TO INTERPRET THE BIBLE, WHY IS IT IMPORTANT TO PAY ATTENTION TO ELEMENTS THAT ARE CRUCIAL IN INTERPRETING ANY E-MAIL, NAMELY: WHO IS THE SENDER? WHO IS THE RECEIVER? AND WHAT DOES THE MESSAGE MEAN?

Working with e-mails gives us helpful clues or tips on valuable skills for interpreting biblical texts. The recipient of an e-mail is unique in their own experience, background, ethnic group, intelligence, and various other factors that come into play when they try to discern what to do or say, or how to respond to whatever comes their way.

When this receiver gets e-mails that are ambiguous and not clear either in content or intent, the person takes steps to interpret what they have received. Whenever the receiver gets such e-mails, the first thing that needs to be assessed is the text.

What is the content of the message that one has received? Where did this message come from? What was the intent of the one who sent it? How much is known about the background and context of this message? How does one understand the message, and how do they react to it? One needs to know as much as possible about the text, most especially the intent and motives of the sender; otherwise, one runs the risk of misinterpreting or misreading the text.

This same process is crucial when it comes to interpreting a biblical text. All one has is the text on the printed page. If one is to understand the text effectively, one needs some background knowledge about the author and community that produced the text. What was the situation and need that led them to write this text? What were they trying to communicate about themselves, God, others, and the world through this text? What means did they use to get this message across? How has this text been read and understood in the past? How do I, as a unique reader in this time and place, understand, interpret, and apply this text to my understanding of self, God, others, and the world? This interpretive process is imperative if we are to avoid the danger of reading into the text what we think is there, instead of what the author and community actually wanted to say to us.

Try using this method the next time you read a particular book or Bible passage. Biblical commentaries, dictionaries, study bibles, and other study aids are readily available to aid in this interpretive venture.

WHAT IS THE APOCRYPHA? WHY DO DIFFERENT VERSIONS OF THE BIBLE CONTAIN DIFFERENT BOOKS?

Apocrypha is a generic Greek word meaning "things that are hidden." When applied to Scripture, it means books that were accepted by some groups but not all. It was applied by both Jews and Christians to writings that were eventually considered not inspired by God, and thus not worthy of being included in the Bible. The list of books that are considered authentic or inspired is usually referred to as the canon of the Bible. Soon the word *apocrypha* took on the connotation of "false, inauthentic, or writings not inspired by God."

Between 150 and 200 AD, the Jews in Palestine were considering what books would officially be included in their canon. One of their criteria was to exclude any books that had been written in Greek. However, Jews outside Palestine used a Greek translation of the Old Testament known as the Septuagint, which included books originally written in Greek. These books were rejected by the Jews when they decided on the definitive material to include in the Hebrew Scriptures, or what we refer to as the Old Testament. They began referring to the rejected books as apocryphal.

Early Christians who had been using the Septuagint translation of the Old Testament accepted these additional books as inspired. They referred to them as deuterocanonical, meaning "second canon." There were many other books written by Christians that were eventually rejected as not inspired. When the definitive list of the New Testament was developed, these Christian books were not included. Writings such as the Gospel of James and the Gospel of Thomas came to be called apocryphal.

During the Protestant Reformation, which began with Martin Luther in 1517, reformers began translating the Bible from the languages in which they were originally written into the native language in use by the reader. The translators noticed the differences between the Jewish and Christian canons of the Old Testament and chose the Jewish canon as more authentic. Thus, they did not accept the books added into the Christian canon as authentic, calling them apocrypha.

So when using the word *apocrypha* for a particular book, it is important to know that various religious groups define the term differently. Jews, Catholics, and other Christians each have books they consider apocryphal.

When the term *apocrypha* is used by Protestants, it usually refers to those seven books of the Old Testament that are not accepted by them or by the Jews. Catholics accept these books as inspired, referring to them as deuterocanonical or "second canon" books. There are also apocryphal books such as the Gospel of Thomas that no Christians, including Catholics, accept as inspired.

While all this may be rather confusing, it is important to know the distinctions, especially in an age when most Bible translations are done in collaboration with Catholics and other Christians, as well as Jews.

The following list includes books or portions of books called apocryphal by Jews and other Christians. Catholics refer to them as deuterocanonical.

The Deuterocanonical Books	
BOOKS	ADDITIONS TO BOOKS IN THE ACCEPTED CANON
Tobit	Additions to Esther
Judith	Letter of Jeremiah
1 Maccabees	Additions to Daniel:
2 Maccabees	The Prayer of Azariah
Wisdom of Solomon	Song of the Three Young Men
Ecclesiaticus or Sirach	Men
Baruch	Susanna
	Bel and the Dragon

2
Historical Tidbits and the Bible

WHO IS ST. JEROME, AND WHY IS HE SO SIGNIFICANT FOR BIBLICAL STUDIES?

Biblical scholars and translators owe a great debt to the model and standard that St. Jerome (345–420) set for all biblical scholarship. Jerome was considered the greatest biblical scholar of his day, conversant with Latin, Greek, and Hebrew. He set about translating the books of the Bible from their original languages into Latin.

Much of Jerome's correspondence with his contemporaries has survived and gives us a glimpse into the kind of person that he was, as well as the time in which he lived. His correspondence with Augustine is of great value in understanding more about both men.

Jerome eventually became Pope Damasus's (366–84) personal secretary. In the West, Latin was overtaking Greek as the language of the common people. The pope desired an accurate translation of the Bible from the original languages into the language and idiom of the people. Previous Latin translations existed, but they were poor in quality.

Jerome set about this task and spent the rest of his life doing it. He is credited with the Bible version known as the Vulgate, a meticulous Latin translation intended to address the needs of the common people. That translation became the standard, and it was from the Vulgate that the Douay-Rheims Bible was translated, the only one used by English-speaking Catholics until modern times.

Catholic Christians did not actively engage in a similar process of providing Scripture in the languages of the people until 1943. Pius XII allowed Catholic scholars once again to go back to the original languages and translate an accurate and meticulous version of the Bible into the languages in use around the world.

Vatican II encouraged Bible translations that reflect the idiom and uniqueness of the ethnic groups using the Bibles. Translations commissioned by various bishops' conferences were developed that reflect the cultural and dynamic equivalence of that conference's particular language. In the United States the bishops commissioned the New American Bible, which is the translation used in all of our liturgical celebrations. The French bishops commissioned the Jerusalem Bible for their people. The tradition of Scripture translation into languages actively in use around the world continues to this day.

WHY, WHEN, AND BY WHOM WAS THE BIBLE DIVIDED INTO CHAPTERS AND VERSES?

When the books of the Bible were originally written, they did not contain chapter or verse references. Early copies of the text were written in continuous columns, often with no breaks or grammatical marks to indicate stops or separations. This proved to be rather cumbersome when it came to referencing the Bible. A method gradually was devised to ease referencing of a particular portion of Scripture. The Bible was divided into chapters and verses to facilitate quick and easy access to biblical passages. It is much easier to find "John, chapter 3, verse 16," than to find "for God so loved the world…" Overall, the chapter and verse divisions are helpful and certainly facilitate easy access to Scripture passages.

The chapter divisions commonly used today were developed by Stephen Langton, an Archbishop of Canterbury. Langton put the modern chapter divisions into place around 1227 AD. The Wycliffe English Bible of 1382 was the first Bible to use this chapter pattern. Since the Wycliffe Bible, nearly all Bible translations have followed Langton's chapter divisions.

The Hebrew Scripture, or the Christian Old Testament, was divided into verses by a Jewish rabbi, Isaac Nathan, in 1448 AD. Robert Estienne, a printer, also known as Stephanus, was the first to divide the New Testament into standard numbered verses in 1551. Stephanus used Nathan's verse divisions for the Old Testament. The first Bible to use the present verse divisions in both testaments is Stephanus's printing of the Latin Vulgate Bible of 1555. Since that time, the chapter and verse divisions employed by Stephanus have been accepted into nearly all Bible versions.

WHAT IMPACT DID POPES LEO XIII AND PIUS XII HAVE ON CATHOLIC BIBLICAL STUDIES? HOW DOES THIS STILL AFFECT US TODAY?

Pope Leo XIII (1810–1903) wrote a papal letter known as an encyclical in 1893 titled *Providentissimus Deus* (the "God of all providence"). He published it on September 30, the feast of St. Jerome, the greatest biblical scholar of the early church. Leo wrote his papal letter at a time when scientific studies and methods were questioning the historical nature and factual accuracy of some Bible passages.

In addressing these concerns, Leo XIII reiterated the longstanding position of the church concerning the inerrancy of the Bible, affirming its historical nature and factual accuracy because of his belief that the Bible was God's Word coming directly from God. Leo could not accept the fact that scientific and historical methods of studying the Bible could be compatible with Catholic authoritative teaching and dogma. He felt that only the church's authoritative teachers could interpret the Bible correctly. Thus biblical scholars were not allowed to differ from or go against the authoritative interpretation of the Bible affirmed by church authorities.

While Leo did offer a slight glimmer of hope in recommending that scholars use and explore scientific methods in studying the Scriptures, they were always subject to the interpretation of the text given by the church. Leo encouraged more extensive use of the Bible by Catholics and even established the Pontifical Biblical Commission to address all matters pertaining to the study and understanding of the Bible.

Fifty years later, on September 30, 1943, Pius XII issued a landmark encyclical titled *Divino Afflante Spiritu* ("Inspired by the Divine Spirit"). In it, Pius gave Catholic biblical scholars official permission to study the biblical text using all the best historical and scientific tools available. Scholars were highly encouraged to go back to the original languages and translate accurately from them. The historical and cultural contexts from which the biblical texts originated were to be explored to give greater clarity and precision to the original intention of the community that produced these texts. The literary forms used, as well as the original sources of the text, were to be analyzed. Both the divine and human dimensions of the Scriptures were to be examined, leading to a more fruitful understanding of the text and its meaning for us today. The method developed to address all these concerns came to be called the "historical-critical" method, which was both highly praised as well as severely criticized by various members of the church.

Vatican II issued its constitution on divine revelation titled *Dei Verbum* (the "Word of God"). The document affirmed in a positive manner all that biblical scholars had begun to do under Pius XII, namely, using all the scientific and historical tools available to understand and interpret the text. This positive focus began to rain down upon all Catholics, leading to a veritable explosion of interest in Bible study, devotional reading, and faith sharing. This thrust was augmented by the revision of the Lectionary, exposing Catholics to more Scripture than ever in the contexts of all liturgical celebrations.

Today, Catholic scholars, both men and women, are at the forefront of biblical scholarship, working collaboratively with other Christians, as well as with Jewish biblical scholars. On local parish levels, this explosion in biblical studies has been met with an equal passion and interest. Much still needs to be done to entice Catholics to read and study the Bible, but significant strides have been made. Hopefully we will all continue to grow in our knowledge and understanding of Scripture, challenged onward by a motto of St. Jerome that "ignorance of the scriptures is ignorance of Christ." Let us all pray that we continue to grow in our knowledge of Christ by familiarizing ourselves with the Scriptures.

1. How do you immerse yourself in the Scriptures?
2. Name times and contexts when Scripture came alive for you.
3. Try using and reflecting on the Sunday readings as a way of preparing yourself to enter more deeply into the Eucharistic celebration.

3
The Bible Before Jesus

WHAT IS THE TORAH—THE KEY FOCUS OF JEWISH LAW, TEACHINGS, TRADITIONS, AND COMMANDMENTS —AND WHICH IS ALSO KNOWN AS THE PENTATEUCH?

When one opens the Bible, the first five books that one encounters are Genesis, Exodus, Leviticus, Numbers, and Deuteronomy. They are called the Torah, or the Law, by Jews, while Christians refer to them as the Pentateuch, or the five books. For Jews, these books are the heart of the Scriptures. The prophetic books always recall the covenant of the Torah between God and humanity, stressing fidelity to the covenantal obligations that the people have distorted or forgotten. Other biblical books always have the Torah as their primary backdrop, either expanding or developing its fundamental ideas and insights.

Genesis 1–11 is considered a prehistory to the beginning of the Jewish people. These chapters recount the creation, the fall in the Garden of Eden, the developing estrangement from God, the flood destroying all living creatures, the rescue of Noah and his family, the rebuilding of the human race, the tower of Babel, and the dispersion of the entire human family.

Genesis 12 and following chapters tell of the call of Abraham to the land of Canaan, and the beginning of the Jewish ancestral traditions through Isaac, Jacob, and his twelve sons. Genesis ends with Jacob's family moving to Egypt at the behest of his son Joseph, who had succeeded, with God's help, in saving both Egypt and his family from famine and starvation.

Exodus begins with the Hebrews in Egypt over 400 years after Joseph. They have grown tremendously in numbers, and the new Egyptian pharaoh or king fears them and enslaves them. As the Hebrews cry out to God for freedom, God prepares a man named Moses for the mission of liberating and saving his people from Egyptian slavery. The rest of the book recounts Moses' dealing with Pharaoh to liberate the people, and Moses' leading the people through the desert to Mount Sinai, where God enters into a covenant with the people, giving them the Law and promising a covenant relationship.

Leviticus and Numbers continue detailing the laws and prescriptions that God revealed at Sinai, along with recounting the continuing adventures of the Hebrews on their journey through the desert to the Promised Land of Canaan. Deuteronomy brings closure to the desert journey. The people are about to enter the Promised Land. Moses, knowing that he will not enter the land, gathers the people and gives them his farewell address. Moses admonishes the people to be faithful to the covenant with God, if they are to be successful in the land they are about to enter. If they are not faithful, God will take the land away from them and punish them. So Moses advises continuous fidelity to the covenant. Once he has finished his address to the people, Moses dies and is buried, while Joshua takes over the leadership as they enter the land that God had given them.

The Torah, or the Pentateuch, recounts the foundational experience of the Jewish people. These five books are the ultimate expression of what Jews have come to know about their God, about themselves as God's people, and about the mutual responsibilities that God's covenant and Law place upon them. Jewish identity, values, perspective, and faith life are beautifully captured in the narrative that these five books relate. These books continually impact Jewish life and identity to this very day.

1. How do you experience narratives from the Torah, especially when read during our Sunday celebrations?
2. Seek out a Jewish person and ask them to explain the significance that the Torah plays in their lives.
3. Compare and contrast the ways in which Christians and Jews understand and articulate the Torah.

WHAT ARE THE HISTORICAL BOOKS OF THE OLD TESTAMENT?

The historical books of the Old Testament recount the events from the time of Joshua to the time of the Maccabees. This covers the centuries from the Hebrew's entrance into the Promised Land in roughly 1200 BCE until 165 BCE and their overthrow of the Greeks who had captured and dominated the land of Israel for centuries. While recounting history in one sense, these books are primarily narratives told from the perspective of covenant fidelity. Fidelity to covenant promises is the lens that focuses all of Jewish history to this day.

Joshua narrates the entrance into the Promised Land and the military strife that the people endured under him in order to capture and maintain the land. By the end of the book, Joshua has conquered the land and has divided the land among the twelve tribes of Israel.

Judges picks up after the death of Joshua. The land consists of twelve tribal entities that are loosely connected. Whenever there is a danger to the people, God sends a leader to take care of the crisis. These people are referred to as judges. They take care of the crisis and then return to their previous way of life. The crisis is usually understood as a punishment from God for not being faithful to the covenant promises made between God and the Hebrew people.

Ruth, a short story of a romantic nature, is placed here because it begins by stating that the events take place during the time of the Judges. It serves primarily as an interlude to the historical narratives. It will ultimately have significance in being connected to the family ancestry of Jesus in the New Testament.

First and **Second Samuel** narrate the story of the last and the greatest of the judges, Samuel, a man who is attentive to God's service and continually challenges the people to covenant fidelity. The people desire a king like their neighboring lands, and petition Samuel and God to give them a king. After many warnings concerning the nature of kings, Samuel reluctantly agrees and anoints first Saul, who soon proves to be a great failure, and then David, the greatest of all of Israel's kings. The rest of these books recount the rise of David as king, along with his many successes and failures. They end with the death of David, succeeded by his son Solomon.

First and **Second Kings** continue the narrative begun in the books of Samuel, beginning with the reign of Solomon, the wise king, who was initially blessed by God until he violated covenant promises by allowing his many wives to influence him to introduce and worship other gods in the land. Upon the death of Solomon, the twelve tribes, which had been united into one kingdom, split into two. The ten tribes of the North became known as Israel, and the two tribes of the South as Judah. The successive kings of both divided kingdoms were summarily judged on the basis of whether they had been faithful to God's covenant promises. Most of them were found wanting. Eventually the Northern Kingdom falls captive to Assyria in 721, and all Hebrews are exiled from the land. The South is spared capture then, but in 586, they are defeated by the Babylonians and are exiled to Babylonia.

First and **Second Chronicles** repeat most of the narratives from Samuel and Kings but from a different perspective. They end with the account of the Babylonian exile.

Ezra and **Nehemiah** narrate the return of the Hebrew people to the Promised Land after the Babylonians are defeated by the Persians under Cyrus's leadership. The books tell of the difficulty the people had in rebuilding the Temple, restoring life to the land, and renewing fidelity to the covenant.

Tobit, Judith, and **Esther** are beautifully crafted stories offering us models of people who struggled in their own situations to remain faithful to covenant promises. All three narrate what fidelity to God can accomplish in one's life.

First and **Second Maccabees** bring the historical books to an end with the account of the Maccabean revolt against the Greeks. Again the main lens through which the events are narrated is that of covenant fidelity. The Maccabees are successful because they were faithful to the covenant, always focused on remaining true to Jewish identity, belief, and practices.

This outline of the historical books manifests the reality that events of life are to be perceived and understood from a faith perspective of covenant fidelity to God. Only this matters. All else is subject to and judged by this criteria.

1. How does your faith life affect the way you perceive and judge the events happening in and around you?
2. Name some examples of this from your personal, social, political, or religious interactions in the world.

WHAT ARE THE WISDOM BOOKS OF THE OLD TESTAMENT? WHAT ISSUES DO THEY ADDRESS?

The Bible's wisdom books are Job, Psalms, Proverbs, Ecclesiastes, and the Song of Songs. These books arise out of that wonderful tendency of human beings to reflect on their experience and to share the insight and wisdom gained from it. Many of life's perplexing experiences and riddles also drive communities to reflect on the meaning of life. The wisdom gained from a particular community's reflection is passed down from one generation to the next, usually in the form of stories, images, or pithy sayings known as proverbs, capturing the wisdom of the ancients. Proverbs are usually unique within every culture and ethnic group, because each one's lived experience is different. At the same time, the insights and wisdom contained in these saying have a universal quality to them because human experience and reflection on life's many riddles have a universal quality. The images and stories might be unique, but the message communicated usually has a universal appeal.

The Jewish people developed their own wisdom tradition, but they also borrowed much from the wisdom traditions of their neighbors and of the nations that often occupied them. There was much to learn from the wisdom traditions of Egypt, Babylonia, Sumeria, and other nations, and Israel did not hesitate to borrow and make that wisdom their own.

The unique feature that Israel contributed to the wisdom tradition is attributing all of wisdom to God, the ultimate source of insights for the whole human family. Wisdom is often personified as a woman who was with God from the very first moment of creation, helping God suffuse all of creation with special divine wisdom. As a result of this connection, "she" takes great delight in all of life and creation, attributing to God the great wonder and joy that all creation brings.

The wisdom traditions also tackle many life issues that have perplexed people for generations, centering mostly on issues of justice: human beings acting with justice toward one another, along with God's justice toward humans. When one experiences the brutal reality of innocent people suffering unjustly, one questions how an all-powerful

God would allow this. Questions arise about how fair life truly is.

Wisdom traditions derived from a variety of sources, especially from the wisdom of tribal or family elders, who were usually considered great sources of wisdom due to their lived experience. Usually these family elders inherited the wisdom that had been handed down from generations past. For those who could afford it, education was also a source for learning and exposure to the wisdom of other cultures and traditions. The ultimate source of much wisdom was the reflection on life that came through personal experience.

Because of their mutual concern with justice, wisdom and prophetic literature share some similar concerns. They emphasize personal responsibility for actions of justice or injustice, along with concerns about how to relate to God and others in terms of what God desires of us. While showing little or no concern toward Israel's history or commandments, wisdom consistently focuses on questions of injustice, the suffering of the innocent, inequality, the unfairness of life, the meaning of life and death, how we are to live, and how we are to relate to God.

1. Reflect on the wisdom about life you have inherited. Give thanks to your family elders who took the time to hand down that wisdom to you.
2. What wisdom will you hand on to your descendants?

WHAT ARE THE PSALMS?

The Old Testament Book of Psalms is a varied collection of Jewish prayers that were intended to be sung and/or prayed publicly during the community's worship and celebration. Most likely they originated for group worship, often within the context of the temple rituals and liturgy.

The Book of Psalms is a collection of 150 psalms, made up of smaller groups of psalms clustered around either similar key themes or similar places. Sometimes a collection was clustered around a particular person whom tradition acknowledged as the author, such as David. The book is organized into five parts, possibly to mirror the five books of the Old Testament known as the Torah. The final editor of the book clearly indicates when each section ends and another begins. The ending of each of the five sections is a prayer of praise and thanksgiving to God, usually known as a doxology. The five collections consist of:

1. Psalms 1–41, with the concluding doxology at Psalm 41:14
2. Psalms 41–72, with the concluding doxology at Psalm 72:18–19
3. Psalms 73–89, with the concluding doxology at Psalm 89:53
4. Psalms 90–106, with the concluding doxology at Psalm 106:48
5. Psalms 107–150, with the concluding doxology at Psalm 150

In Hebrew, the Book of Psalms is called the *Tehillim*, the book of praises to God. This continual praising of God occurs in the midst of all the variety of positive and negative experiences, events and emotions of life. Each and every event of life's ordinary, routine, and unremarkable passage becomes an occasion to give God praise. Prayers of praise and thanksgiving to God are intimately connected to occasions when sadness, lament, and anguish dominate the human experience. In the midst of life's gamut of emotions, experiences, and concerns, God is to be trusted and praised.

From the very beginning of the Christian community's prayer life, the psalms have held a special place. They were and still are continually prayed, sung, and reflected in the prayer life of the Christian community. This form of prayer and reflection on the psalms is known in the Christian tradition as the Liturgy of the Hours. The day is broken into periods of time known as "hours" during which one stops everything to praise God by reciting or singing the psalms.

Psalms reveal the close connection that the Jews had and still have with God. There is a freshness to the psalms that arises from being in intimate relationship with God. A Jew in a covenant relationship with God could be angry at God, could be thankful of God, or could even try to persuade God to see things differently. But one thing that a Jew could never do was *avoid* God. Psalms capture that very deep covenant love that the Jews experience in their relationship with God. When we pray the psalms, we, too, enter into that depth of relationship with God that governs all of life's experiences.

HOW DOES ONE CREATE A PERSONAL PSALM?

Take time to enter into the psalm prayer experience by creating your own psalm. The suggestion here uses the pattern of the Responsorial Psalm in Mass.

Complete one or more of the following verses. To enter the psalm prayer experience, begin with the refrain, and then repeat the refrain after every verse you have completed.

Refrain: We praise you, O Lord, for all your works are wonderful.

We praise you, O Lord, forever is your love

I praise you, God, for…

Refrain

I have a complaint, God, about…

Refrain

I am concerned, O God, about…

Refrain

I thank you, God, for…

Refrain

I place in your hands, O God…

Refrain

WHO ARE THE PROPHETS AND WHAT WAS THEIR ROLE?

The Old Testament contains various books that are called prophetic books. There are major prophets, such as Isaiah, Jeremiah, and Ezekiel, as well as minor prophets, such as Amos, Hosea, and Micah.

The popular understanding of prophets and prophecy portrays them as concerned with predicting future events. Those predictions are also understood in terms of God's punishment on people who are not doing what is expected of them. While this may be partly true, it is not the best interpretation of prophets and prophecy in the Bible. There is no denial that prophets talk about future consequences and sometimes say something that appears like a prediction of the future. But in reality, prophets are primarily concerned with the here and now. They are people who seem to be more and better attuned than others around them to the ethical and moral situation of their community.

Prophets have a sense of being called by God to speak to the people on God's behalf. A deep sense of relationship with and understanding of God's purposes and intentions motivates them to address the people in words that usually begin with the phrase, "Thus says the Lord…" This stance demands a spirituality that is continually attuned to God's desires and intentions.

While prophets may seem to focus on gloom and doom, their primary intent is to communicate to people God's continued love and concern for them. They continually remind the community of God's desire from the very beginning to enter into a love relationship with them. God chose them and they accepted that choice, promising fidelity and faithfulness in that relationship. Prophets consistently remind people of that relationship, especially as they become aware that the community has departed from its original sense of faithfulness.

This special vocation demands the development of "eyes" that can see deeper than most people see. It demands a sensitive moral "nose" that can detect what is not right in the community's relationship with God and with others. It demands a set of developed "ears" that attune to what God is saying about the current lived experience of the community. These developed "senses" allow the prophet to become a champion for justice, continually alerting the community to violations of what is right and just for those claiming to be God's chosen people.

Feeling compelled to speak on God's behalf no matter what the consequences, prophets call people to repentance, to justice, and to a realignment of their priorities and values. Consequently, prophets are often rejected, abused, persecuted, killed, and even more often, totally ignored.

1. Who has played the role of prophet in your life?
2. In the life of your community?
3. Whom would you list as a modern-day prophet who speaks on behalf of those who have no voice?

What is apocalyptic literature, and how does it impact both the Old and the New Testaments?

During times of severe difficulties in life or the world, people often feel overwhelmed by circumstances and powerless to do anything about them. In the middle of such oppressive circumstances, people often turn to God, asking questions like, Where is God? Why is God allowing such things to happen? If these difficulties remain over a long period of time, faith-filled people's relationship to God begins to take on a certain flavor. In biblical terms this "flavor" is known as an apocalyptic way of thinking, which eventually leads to an apocalyptic way of writing. Thus, apocalyptic literature surfaces from life situations and contexts that involve deep suffering and/or persecution.

In many ways, apocalyptic writing is related to the prophetic tradition; it is concerned about God's viewpoint, role, and presence in the actual events of life. However, the style and form that apocalyptic thinking takes is definitely different from the prophetic style.

Apocalyptic writing is intended as a means of offering hope, consolation, support, and strength to all who suffer, especially to all who feel they suffer unjustly. The apocalyptic mindset presents to all suffering people a God who is still very much present and attuned to what is happening. Our God is still in charge, despite appearances to the contrary. One day soon our God is going to put certain plans and events into place that will eliminate the injustice and suffering we are experiencing. God will deal with those who have brought about such injustice and suffering. Our role is to trust that our God continues to care, and to hold on to that hope no matter how bad things get. Eventually, God will intervene and all will be righted. What is needed now is trust, hope, perseverance, patience, and total reliance on God.

Those writing apocalyptic literature state that God has revealed such plans to them through visions, angels, dreams, or other intermediaries. By these means, apocalyptic writers have come to know of God's plans, care, and concern about what is happening. They in turn reveal those plans to those who have faith and who believe so that they may continue to have hope and perseverance. The language used to communicate such visions and plans tends to be highly symbolic. The meaning is understood only by those who share inside knowledge and information, while remaining hidden and confusing to those who do not know.

The apocalyptic mindset and literature tend to see human actions and events from a pessimistic perspective. They do not believe that anything can be done about the current realities because the hand of the evil one, or Satan, is at work, and no human power can override the present reality. But someday soon there will be a final struggle between the forces of evil and the forces of good. God, leading the forces of good, will eventually win out, and peace, harmony, justice, and an end to all forms of suffering will be realized. Those who have been faithful and who have persevered will experience this rich new reality and will relish in it, while the evil ones will be punished.

The best example of apocalyptic writing in the Bible is the Book of Revelation, the last book in the New Testament and in the whole Bible. Apocalyptic influences are evident in all four Gospels, as well as in the Old Testament Book of Daniel, especially chapters 7–12, and that of Ezekiel.

1. Briefly describe a time of great suffering, pain, or persecution that you have experienced in your life.
2. How do some of the key themes surfaced by apocalyptic writing offer hope, strength, and courage to endure through such times?
3. How was your relationship to God during that time?
4. What was the form and content of your prayers to God during this time?

4

Communities of Faith That Produced the Gospels

WHAT PROCESS LED TO THE DEVELOPMENT OF THE GOSPELS?

The *Catechism of the Catholic Church*, #126, states:

> We can distinguish three stages in the formation of the Gospels: 1. The life and teaching of Jesus...; 2. The oral tradition...; 3. The written Gospels...

The writing of the Gospels begins with the experience of Jesus, a first-century male Jew who preaches the kingdom of God to his fellow Jews in a way that challenges them to a deeper living of their covenant with God. Jesus understands God in a broader and more expansive manner than some of his fellow Jews. Breaking down social and religious boundaries that separate outcasts and sinners from God's love and concern is something that Jesus actively demonstrates both in his teaching and in his way of living. Jesus challenges the followers he attracts to build the kingdom of God on earth by living life attuned to the needs of others, most especially the poor, the outcasts, and the marginalized. In his words and his deeds, Jesus always manifests God's love for all. This lifestyle eventually gets Jesus into trouble with religious and political authorities of his day. They eventually arrest him and crucify him, assured that they had rid themselves of another Jewish troublemaker.

That is not the end of the story. His followers soon experience him as being alive and active in their midst. This experience leads them to reflect deeply on all that Jesus said, did, and meant to them while he was with them. As they reflect on the meaning of Jesus' life, passion, death, and resurrection, they share those reflections with others who are willing to listen. Thus begins the oral tradition concerning who Jesus was and what he meant to the communities that saw him as a model for how to relate to God and others.

That oral tradition first tried to make sense of who Jesus was and what it meant that he had died and yet was experienced as alive. The people understood Jesus to be God's Messiah, who, though killed for his radical teaching and lifestyle, was raised up by God and proclaimed Lord. Jesus' resurrection was understood as God's seal of approval on Jesus' teaching and way of living, calling his followers to continue carrying out his vision and mission. Soon, telling the oral story of Jesus began to take on a certain format and outline. It included, in this order:

1. The ministry of John the Baptist
2. Jesus' public ministry soon after John is arrested

3. Jesus' ministry in Galilee
4. His journey to Judea
5. His controversy with the leaders in Jerusalem
6. His eventual passion, death, and resurrection

As the followers of Jesus continued to share the good news of Jesus' resurrection, people who knew nothing about Jesus asked all sorts of questions concerning their own life situations. Jesus' followers developed responses to these questions and concerns by detailing Jesus' teachings and deeds, and how they could be applied to people's circumstances and life situations. Soon collections of such responses appeared, containing Jesus' parables, miracles, sayings, and deeds. Much of this material was collected in both oral and written form, but there was not yet a systematic account of Jesus' sayings and deeds. The letters of Paul come into being, all written before any Gospel was ever penned.

Between 67 and 73 AD, the first systematic account of Jesus' ministry was penned by an author known as Mark. Mark addressed a community that was being rejected and persecuted for its belief in Jesus. In the Gospel According to Mark, Jesus, in the context of his ministry, emphasizes that following him demands great sacrifice and involves suffering and persecution. Mark narrates Jesus' ministry as a struggle with the forces of evil, picturing Jesus as the suffering servant of God who was willing to endure even the cross to be faithful to God's values, purposes, and intentions.

About 85 AD, possibly in Antioch in Syria, another author penned a systematic account of Jesus' ministry. Eventually known as the Gospel According to Matthew, this Jesus account is addressed primarily to a Jewish audience, stressing the reality that Jesus was the long awaited Messiah promised in the Scriptures. According to Matthew, Jesus, a righteous Jew, came to renew his people, challenging them to be faithful to the covenant promises while deepening and expanding their understanding of those promises.

Also written around 85 AD, the Gospel According to Luke, along with the Acts of the Apostles, addresses a community that is primarily Gentile, that is, non-Jewish. The message that Luke wants to convey to his community is the good news of Jesus, the universal savior of all people, most especially the poor, the marginalized, and the alienated.

The Gospel According to John, penned sometime around 95 AD, speaks to a community that is in conflict over the true identity of Jesus. Who Jesus was, why he came, and what he accomplished in their midst were major sources of conflict within John's community. John presents Jesus as the divine one in our midst, come to bring life and light to the world and to any who risk following him.

There were many other gospels written, but the early communities chose these four as faithful and authentic witnesses to the mission and ministry of Jesus. By knowing and understanding Jesus' mission and values, every generation can apply that mission and those values to its particular life situation and context.

1. Reflect on how you apply Jesus' mission, ministry, and values to the unique context of your life and community.
2. Share some concrete examples of how we do this today, facing moral issues and situations that Jesus never faced or never addressed.

WHAT IS THE MIND AND HEART OF THE COMMUNITY THAT PRODUCED THE GOSPEL ACCORDING TO MARK?

A gospel is a narrative of the life and ministry of Jesus, addressed to a particular faith community. Each gospel community had particular needs and concerns that arose out of their unique context or situation. Years after Jesus had lived, died, risen from the dead, and returned to the Father, the community needed guidance in how to make Jesus' message relevant to their own lived experience. Each gospel author attempted the task of concretizing Jesus' life and message for his particular community. In their narratives, they reflected their community's faith in Jesus.

Mark, the first canonical Gospel to be written, is dated somewhere between 67 and 73 AD. When Matthew and Luke wrote their Gospels a decade or so later, they adapted Mark's for their communities, because the needs and concerns of their communities were different from those of Mark.

Mark's Gospel seems to be addressed to a faith community that is undergoing turmoil, rejection, suffering, and persecution for being disciples of Jesus. These forces threaten to overwhelm them, possibly leading to division and dissolution of the community. Mark wanted to help people plagued by doubt and fear to respond with faith and a life of discipleship. This context provides Mark the parameters around which he fashions the story of Jesus.

Mark presents Jesus as the one sent by God to confront the forces of evil that threaten anyone who chooses to be a follower of Jesus. Mark's Jesus often says little, but is continually on the move, doing things that comfort, console, heal, reconcile, and challenge. Following the announcement of his vocational mission at his baptism, Jesus is driven by the Spirit into the desert, where he encounters the forces of evil. Mark presents Jesus as the strong one who returns victorious over the forces of evil, ready to confront all those forces that oppose the will of God and the establishment of God's reign on earth. This is the good news that Jesus brings to a suffering world undergoing turmoil. Jesus models for us how to encounter, overcome, and finally defeat such evil forces. Foremost is the conviction that God is our sure source of strength and help in this struggle.

Mark's image of Jesus, and consequently of any disciple of Jesus, is that of the suffering servant. Jesus' struggle with demonic forces leads to confrontation, rejection, and outright opposition. Because Jesus presents a threat, the evil forces conspire to do away with him. Jesus is not deterred. Rather, he calls for total faith in God who helps us to overcome the forces of evil.

Such faith, however, does not remove the consequences of battling evil forces. Jesus endures rejection, abuse, persecution, suffering, and even death. He is ultimately arrested, tortured, and crucified in his battle with the demonic forces.

Yet, this is not the end. Through the suffering servant, the one who suffers for the sake of others, redemption and salvation will come to all. Mark ends with the announcement of the good news of Jesus' resurrection. The resurrection becomes God's seal of approval on the lifestyle and the vocation of Jesus. In the resurrection, Jesus' apparent defeat is transformed by God into resurrected life that will continue forever. Such will also be the fate of all who, like Jesus, struggle against the forces of evil operative in their lives and communities.

For Mark, following Jesus in faithful discipleship demands tremendous faith in God, our source of power and strength in the continual battle for good against the forces of evil. This struggle demands much of the disciple. Disciples can delude themselves into thinking that the struggle is not as bad as it seems. This blindness can be debilitating. For Mark, Jesus is the only one who can remove our blindness. This is done most effectively by following Jesus, modeling our lives on his, always aware that the forces of evil continually conspire against the good. If we live our lives in fidelity to the model of Jesus, we can rest assured that, no matter what happens, God will bring new meaning and new life to all that we do.

1. How do you strive to remove whatever blinds you from following the challenging and difficult path that Jesus has forged?

WHAT IS THE MIND AND HEART OF THE COMMUNITY THAT PRODUCED THE GOSPEL ACCORDING TO MATTHEW?

To understand Matthew and his message, we must first understand the situation or context of Matthew's community. Matthew is writing for a community that is undergoing a change in identity and direction, much like the Catholic Christian community of today.

Matthew's community is a predominantly Jewish group that has accepted Jesus as the Messiah. They value their identity as Jews and feel that Jesus is what the Torah, prophets, and writings have all been pointing to, the long-awaited Messiah. Yet they are in conflict with other Jews who hold the dominant Jewish viewpoint that Jesus is not the Messiah.

This situation creates a real identity crisis for Matthew's Jewish community. Who are they to believe and follow: Moses, as articulated and interpreted by the Pharisees? Jesus, as articulated and taught by their faith community? Who are the correct, proper, and authoritative teachers, the Pharisees or the disciples of Jesus? The community does not want to reject their Jewishness, for it is the very core of their faith lives. Yet it is a Jewishness that is now viewed through the Jesus lens. What are they to do? How are they to think, feel, act? Matthew's community fashions this gospel story of Jesus to address these crucial issues and concerns.

The flow and sequence of the Gospel of Matthew directly address the concerns of his Jewish community. Matthew begins with a prologue, the first part of which is a genealogy establishing Jesus as a Jew among Jews, from the line of Abraham, a descendent from the house of David, and one in touch with the Jewish experience and spirituality of exile and return. Jesus is a Jew par excellence in touch with the heart of Judaism. Yet Jesus is also identified as Emmanuel, "God with Us," who will accomplish the role of the Messiah to save the people. (The name *Jesus* actually means "God saves.")

This salvation is intended for all of God's people, not just the Jews. As a result Matthew's community must be that living light to which all will be attracted. This will demand great openness, courage, and faith. It will create much tension and stress, forcing the community to let go of secure space and relationships, yet it will eventually yield great fruit. They believe that they are not alone on this journey. Jesus, God with Us, is their constant support and presence for all time. This is the faith stance of Matthew's community, and this is what Matthew wants his fellow Jews to hold on to.

Jesus is presented as the one like Moses who will act on behalf of the people. Matthew highlights Jesus' role as a teacher and a lawgiver, one not merely equal to Moses, but greater, offering the community a deeper and more expansive version of the Torah. Jesus' teachings are consciously edited by Matthew into five major discourses, mirroring and deepening the understanding of the five books of Jewish Law, the Torah.

The Sermon on the Mount highlights the five major discourses that occur in the Gospel (chapters 5–7, 10, 13, 18, 23–25). Jesus not only fills his primary role in Matthew's Gospel as teacher, but he also acts with constant care and concern for others, most especially the least of all people (chapters 8–9, 25).

With diligent care Jesus gathers around him those who will listen and understand all that he says and does, and then are ready to go and do the same. In chapter 10 and especially in 28:18–20, these followers of Jesus are commissioned to carry out to the ends of the earth all that Jesus has said and done. Jesus extends to them the authority given him from the Father, with the assurance that Jesus will be with them till the end of time (again the word play on the title of Jesus as Emmanuel, God with Us).

For Matthew's community, Jesus and his followers are the true, legitimate, authoritative teachers, in line with the best of Judaism, challenging the community to model itself on Jesus, the true teacher of Torah. Jews accepting Jesus as Messiah should have no doubts about the authenticity of Jesus' message and the reliability of his call, for he backs it with divine authority and endless presence in our midst.

This rather structured and organized Gospel was greatly esteemed by the Christian community because of its emphasis on the teaching role of Jesus and his disciples.

Its catechetical clarity made this Gospel an ideal tool in the formation of those interested in coming to know and follow Jesus.

1. How do you maintain hope and trust when others challenge the faith journey that you have chosen?

WHAT IS THE MIND AND HEART OF THE COMMUNITY THAT PRODUCED THE GOSPEL ACCORDING TO LUKE?

The predominant image presented by Luke's community is that of Jesus as Savior of all humanity. Luke is the only Gospel calling Jesus the Savior. Jesus is God made human in order for salvation to be actualized for all humanity. Luke, more than any other Gospel, shows Jesus as one concerned for all, thus making Jesus' mission directed not just to Jews but to all people. This is most clearly expressed by Luke when, in recounting Jesus' genealogy (3:23–37), Luke traces it all the way back to Adam, one of the biblical parents of the whole human race, in contrast to Matthew's genealogy (Matt 1:1–17), which traces Jesus' roots back to Abraham, one of the biblical ancestors of the Jewish nation.

The context of Luke's community seems to be cosmopolitan, with all the diversity that a cosmopolitan urban setting offers. There are Jews and Gentiles, rich and poor, the accepted and the rejected, the mainstream and the marginalized. Amidst this diversity, Luke's Jesus is concerned for all, but seems to have a special concern for the marginalized, the alienated, the poor, the oppressed, and the outcast. Luke also pays special attention to the role of women, and how Jesus' countercultural treatment of them raises their status in an essentially patriarchal society.

Luke's Jesus displays a radical inclusiveness that extends salvation to all, most especially sinners, the poor, the aliens, the Samaritans, the outcasts, and women. Luke continually pictures Jesus as sharing table fellowship with those who would usually not be welcomed. For Luke, Jesus continually breaks down all barriers separating people, especially those of race, creed, gender—inviting all to the table and treating all as equal, even the most despised and rejected of people.

From the moment of his family being unwelcome in Bethlehem, to his birth in a stable, to his being laid in a manger, Luke's Jesus, the Son of God and Savior, experiences what it means to be outcast, poor, homeless, and unwanted.

Luke's own magnificent gift of storytelling presents Jesus relating stories of the Good Samaritan (10:16–23); the loving father and the prodigal son (15:11–32); the rich man and Lazarus (16:19–31); the Pharisee and the tax collector (18:9–14); and Zacchaeus, the tax collector (22:35–38). The main ingredient of all these memorable stories is the need to continually break down the barriers that divide human beings from one another. We cannot do it on our own. Jesus models for us the way to break down barriers, offering his life for the sake of being faithful to that mission. Luke's Jesus is the Savior of all. Through

Luke's gift as a storyteller and a painter of words, we see the heart and mind of Jesus as remembered and experienced by the community for which Luke is writing.

How does Luke's Jesus maintain this focus on radical inclusiveness in his mission and in the face of opposition from the "powers that be," especially some of the religious leadership? Luke's community experienced and remembered Jesus as a person of great faith and prayer, constantly in tune with the prompting and guidance of God's Spirit in his thoughts and actions. Consistently, Jesus refocuses his life and mission through periods of prayer and reflection (5:16; 6:12; 9:18, 28; 10:21–22; 11:1; 22:39–46). Luke's Jesus teaches his disciples to pray and encourages all to pray for strength, guidance, and help in carrying out this mission of radical inclusiveness, and not be tempted to give up on the mission in the face of opposition and rejection.

1. Read Luke's Gospel and note how Jesus models what it means to be an inclusive disciple.
2. How do you practice inclusivity in your interactions with others?

WHAT IS THE MIND, HEART, AND MESSAGE OF THE AUTHOR OF THE GOSPEL ACCORDING TO JOHN?

The Gospel According to John is different from the three Gospels of Matthew, Mark, and Luke. These three are usually referred to as the Synoptic Gospels, or gospels that have a similar pattern, despite their different emphases on the identity, message, and mission of Jesus. John's Gospel, written somewhere between 90 and 100 AD, is different in emphases, structure, style, and content.

The community that produced John's Gospel seems to be primarily Jews who have accepted Jesus as the Messiah. They are in a struggle with Jewish leaders who do not accept Jesus as Messiah and who revile those Jews who do. These followers of Jesus are being thrown out of synagogues and treated as heretics or unfaithful Jews. They exist in constant tension and conflict with their fellow Jews. John's community is in need of clarity because of this conflict. Who is Jesus, and can we trust the path that he came to forge for us? What does turning our life over to Jesus involve? If we go public with our belief in Jesus, what are some possible consequences? What does God really want of us? John writes his Gospel to address these and other major concerns of his community, with the assuring knowledge of Jesus' identity, role, and mission.

For John, Jesus is the Word of God who existed from the very beginning with God. The Word of God became flesh, one of us, by pitching his tent among us, in order to show us the path to God. Images of light in the midst of darkness highlight the identity and mission of Jesus. Lengthy dialogues and monologues give John's Jesus the opportunity to discuss at length his mission and purpose. The seven miracles, or "signs" as John calls them, are intended not only to show the divinity and power of Jesus, but also to allow Jesus to delve into topics concerning faithful discipleship. These signs become the occasions for deeper understanding concerning Jesus' identity and role, as well as for greater awareness of what accepting and following him entails. Some who witness these signs accept them and believe. Others reject these signs and plot against Jesus.

For John, encountering Jesus demands a choice, forcing people to accept or reject, to believe or deny, to live in the light or to remain in darkness. There is no middle ground. Those who reject feel safer in doing away with Jesus and plot to do so. He is eventually arrested and killed. But according to John, this was God's plan all along the way. Jesus' passion and death become the means for Jesus to manifest God's ultimate purpose, to be willing to offer all, most especially himself as God's own Son, for the sake of others. This path does not end in defeat, as others may have desired, but rather becomes the path back to the Father, and to ultimate glory and exaltation. For John, Jesus' crucifixion is at very same time his exaltation. Passion, death, resurrection, ascension, and the sending forth of the Spirit are all one unified reality for John.

John's Gospel pictures Jesus as aware of his divinity and in touch with his Father, both in terms of knowing clearly the Father's will and having the courage, strength, and willingness to carry it out. John consistently has Jesus address key issues that would have been of great concern to his community as they struggled with fellow Jews in their acceptance of Jesus. Images of baptism and open acceptance of Jesus abound in Jesus' encounters with Nicodemus (chapter 3) and the Samaritan women at the well (chapter 4). Conversion images and what openly following Jesus entails are addressed at length in the dialogues concerning the curing of the crippled man (chapter 5) and the blind man (chapter 9). The account of the raising of Lazarus (chapter 10) speaks directly to the issues concerning death, resurrection, and eternal life.

These passages have been consistently used by Christian communities from the very beginning to highlight our faith journey to God. They are still used during the seasons of Lent and Easter, guiding us and anyone who would wish to join us, along the path of conversion, of moving from darkness to light, and to ultimate union with God through death and resurrection.

1. As you read John's Gospel and encounter Jesus, reflect on what attracts you to this presentation of Jesus.
2. Does Jesus become a source of light for you?
3. Does Jesus occasion a deeper understanding of who you are and what you are about?
4. How comfortable are you in being a disciple of Jesus, as portrayed in this Gospel? Give some specifics.

5

What Is the Lectionary?

Vatican II, a reform council of all the world's bishops held
in Rome from 1962 to 1965, called for a revision of the
Lectionary, the book containing all the Scripture readings
used at liturgical celebrations. The thrust of the committee that worked on the revision was to expose Catholics to
more Scripture than they had been exposed to in the
pre–Vatican II Lectionary. That Lectionary consisted of a
one-year cycle with two readings that came exclusively
from the New Testament, the first reading from one of the
New Testament letters and the gospel reading from one of
the four Gospels. The same readings would be repeated
each year.

The committee developed two very significant revi-
sions of that existing Lectionary. The first dealt with the
development of a three-year cycle of readings rather than
a one-year cycle. The second significant revision added a
third reading taken from the Old Testament, along with a
psalm. Appropriate Old Testament passages were selected

based on how they would link to the other readings, as well as how they fit into the liturgical seasons.

A calendar of three complete Lectionary cycles was developed, each focusing on one of the Gospels. The cycles became known as Years A, B, C, focusing on the Gospels of Matthew, Mark, and Luke, respectively. John's Gospel was not given a liturgical cycle since it was decided to maintain its traditional use throughout particular seasons of the year, such as Lent and Easter.

First the Scripture reading from the Gospel for each Sunday was selected and examined. The Old Testament was then explored to see which passage could be found that linked to the Gospel in terms of theme, similarity of language or ideas, or prefiguring of New Testament persons or events. That passage was then chosen, linking it to the Gospel passage and placing it within the context of an appropriate liturgical season.

Liturgically, the Old Testament reading is often interpreted not on its own merits, either historically or culturally, but rather in light of its relationship to the New Testament Scripture. Christ is the focus of our liturgical celebrations, and all the readings are meant to point to Christ and the paschal mystery that the liturgy continually celebrates. Be aware of this approach as you listen to the readings being proclaimed during our Sunday liturgical celebrations.

WHAT ROLE DOES THE RESPONSORIAL PSALM PLAY IN LECTIONARY READINGS FOR ANY GIVEN SUNDAY?

The Responsorial Psalm on any given Sunday is the only one of the four readings that the entire assembly actively proclaims. Usually led by a cantor, the whole assembly is asked to join in the refrain from the psalm while the cantor leads by chanting the selected verses.

The Responsorial Psalm is actually a selection of verses from a psalm that reflects the theme of the readings for that Sunday. As a result, the refrain and the selected verses provide a lens through which one might examine and converse with the other three readings.

Many have found the following process an excellent way of exploring the meaning of the Sunday readings. This process enables us to mine the readings in a way that yields rich resources.

1. Find and read the entire psalm from which the Responsorial Psalm is selected.
2. Determine the psalm's overall message and theme.
3. Notice the verses and the refrain selected for that particular Sunday.
4. What theme is being presented in the refrain and the verses of the Responsorial Psalm?
5. Once a key theme or focus is determined, move to the other readings, keeping in mind the refrain and the theme from the psalm.
6. What focus does the psalm shed on the other readings?

Following this process allows the Responsorial Psalm, which the whole assembly proclaims together, to become the thematic lens that helps unpack the message of God's Word from the other readings.

Try the process for a few Sundays and see if it helps bring a new perspective on the readings that you might not have noticed before.

WHAT ARE THE NEW TESTAMENT LETTERS AND WHAT DID PAUL CONTRIBUTE TO THAT COLLECTION?

Letters comprise the bulk of the New Testament books. Twenty-one of the twenty-seven New Testament books are letters from various people, the bulk of them from Paul or his followers. Letters were an easy and common method of communicating in the ancient world, as they are today. Some letters are more formal than others. Overall, letters tend to have a similar structure consisting of a greeting, the body—which addresses the issues at hand—a conclusion, and a closing. The New Testament letters are attributed to various followers of Jesus, written as they tried to make sense of what Jesus meant to their communities, and how they were to live as a result of having encountered Jesus.

Paul, a Jew who initially persecuted the followers of Jesus, eventually accepted Jesus as the Messiah and began to minister in his name, ultimately spreading his message to both Jews and Gentiles. Paul traveled widely in his evangelizing mission and founded communities wherever he went.

As he traveled to other places, the communities he had founded and given birth to would contact him to ask questions or seek guidance on various issues. Paul would also hear about the status and condition of these communities from people who had visited them. The easiest way for Paul to respond to their concerns was to write letters. Many letters were probably written that have not survived. But the letters in the New Testament have, and they tell us much about Paul, his communities, and their attempts to be faithful to the teaching Paul had imparted to them.

Paul's letters were composed before any Gospel was ever written. There is no tradition or school of theology that Paul could fall back on. Rather, Paul depended on his own keen insights and reflections into the meaning of Jesus for the people of his time. Essentially, Paul was "doing theology" by the seat of his pants, meaning that he was applying Jesus' message to the practical circumstances and problems of his communities, without much tradition or background to fall back upon.

Scholars accept seven of the twenty-one New Testament letters to be authentically written by Paul. They are 1 Thessalonians, 1 and 2 Corinthians, Galatians, Philippians, Philemon, and Romans. Another six are considered to have been written by disciples of Paul, writing in his spirit. These are Colossians, 2 Thessalonians, Ephesians, 1 and 2 Timothy, and Titus. The Letter to the Hebrews, in the past associated with Paul, was written by an unknown author. The last seven of the twenty-one letters are attributed to the apostolic authors noted in their titles: James; Jude; 1 and 2 Peter; and 1, 2, and 3 John.

The second Lectionary reading of each Sunday's Eucharistic celebration proclaims the letters in a somewhat continuous fashion. Each of the three Lectionary years exposes us to selections from different letters, allowing us to enter into the world of the early followers of Jesus. (See table below.) One begins to realize that even though the particulars may be different, the human emotions, struggles, and questions concerning what it means to follow Jesus are perennial.

The next time you celebrate the Sunday liturgy, pay attention to the selection from the New Testament letter. Go to the Bible and locate that letter. Read the introduction to it to learn about its background. Reflect on what that letter is saying to you today about what following Jesus entails.

Lectionary Selections from the New Testament Letters		
Year A	1 Corinthians 1–4	Sundays of the year, weeks 2–8
	Romans	Sundays of the year, weeks 9–24
	Philippians	Sundays of the year, weeks 25–28
	1 Thessalonians	Sundays of the year, weeks 29–33
Year B	1 Corinthians 6–11	Sundays of the year, weeks 2–6
	2 Corinthians	Sundays of the year, weeks 7–14
	Ephesians	Sundays of the year, weeks 15–21
	James	Sundays of the year, weeks 22–26
	Hebrews 1–10	Sundays of the year, weeks 27–33

Continued next page

Continued

Lectionary Selections from the New Testament Letters		
Year C	1 Corinthians 12–15	Sundays of the year, weeks 2–8
	Galatians	Sundays of the year, weeks 9–14
	Colossians	Sundays of the year, weeks 15–18
	Hebrews 11–12	Sundays of the year, week 19–22
	Philemon	Sundays of the year, week 23
	1 Timothy	Sundays of the year, week 24–26
	2 Timothy	Sundays of the year, week 27–30
	2 Thessalonians	Sundays of the year, week 31–33

WHY DOES JOHN'S GOSPEL NOT HAVE ITS OWN LECTIONARY YEAR, THE WAY THE OTHER THREE GOSPELS DO? WHAT ROLE DOES JOHN HAVE IN THE VATICAN II–REVISED LECTIONARY?

Vatican II, an ecumenical council of the church held from 1962 to 1965, called for a revision of the one-year Lectionary, the book containing all the Bible readings proclaimed during liturgical celebrations. There was much discussion by the group designated to work on revising the Lectionary, concerning how to restructure it. Ultimately, a three-year Lectionary was decided upon, primarily structured around the three Synoptic Gospels of Matthew, Mark, and Luke, referred to as Year A, B, and C, respectively. Since there are four Gospels, the question surfaces as to why no Lectionary year is devoted to the Gospel According to John.

The committee working on the revision discussed the issue at length, but decided against it for a variety of reasons. The main reason focused around the reality that John, from the very beginning of the Christian liturgical life, had been used extensively during the seasons of Lent and Easter. The committee wanted to retain that privileged place for John, so decided against a Lectionary year for John's Gospel.

The other major reason centered around the reality that John's Gospel was different from the Synoptics. John contained lengthy monologues and dialogues of Jesus that would have been difficult to break into smaller segments over a Lectionary year. Doing this would have broken up the logic and argumentation of the dialogues and monologues, thus leading to possible confusion or distortion of Jesus' message. The committee saw this as a major obstacle to a Lectionary year devoted to John, and so decided not to go down that path.

Below is a list detailing the Sundays and seasons during which the Gospel of John is proclaimed in the three liturgical years.

SUNDAYS OF THE THREE-YEAR REVISED LECTIONARY

Advent
B—Third Sunday of Advent

Christmas
Christmas Day Mass
Second Sunday after Christmas

Lent

A—Third to Fifth Sunday of Lent
B—Third to Fifth Sunday of Lent
C—Fifth Sunday of Lent

Holy Week

Holy Thursday
Good Friday

Easter

Easter Sunday
A——Second and the Fourth to Seventh Sunday of
    Easter, and Pentecost
B—Second and the Fourth to Seventh Sunday of
    Easter, and Pentecost
C—Second to Seventh Sunday of Easter, and
    Pentecost

Ordinary Time

A—Second Sunday of Ordinary Time
B—Second and the Seventeenth to Twenty-First
    Sunday of Ordinary Time, and Christ the King
C—Second Sunday of Ordinary Time

If you would like to know more about the structure of
the Lectionary and the committee that worked on restruc-
turing it, there is no better work available than *The Sunday
Lectionary* by Normand Bonneau.

1. Reflect on how you experience the Lectionary as you
   celebrate Sunday liturgy.

2. Does its structure make sense to you? (Refer to the other sections of this book that speak about other aspects of the Lectionary.)
3. How would you explain to a friend what the Lectionary is and how it is structured?

6

Faith Traditions and the Bible

CHRISTIAN LECTIONARIES LINK THE BIBLICAL TEXT TO THE LITURGICAL YEAR CYCLES. HOW DOES THIS DIFFER FROM THE WAY OTHER CHRISTIAN DENOMINATIONS READ THE BIBLE?

A lectionary is a ritual book containing select biblical passages taken out of their original context. Connected to other biblical passages by theme or topic, and linked to the liturgical season and feasts, they are read together at weekly community celebrations. Homilies by the presider are to be based on the readings, reflecting on them and making applications to the everyday faith lives of all Christians.

Vatican II (an ecumenical reform council which held sessions at the Vatican from 1962 to 1965) called for a revision of the Mass prayers, as well as the Lectionary then in use. Vatican II's revision of the Lectionary into three liturgical years or cycles was so well received that many of the mainline Christian denominations began using it in their own community celebrations. They tweaked some of the assigned texts to make them applicable to their particular feasts and celebrations, but overall the integrity of the

Lectionary was maintained. That Lectionary is referred to in Christian circles as the Common Lectionary. Today, we find that most Christians read the Bible through the lens of a Lectionary.

Other Christian denominations do not use a lectionary at their communal gatherings. Each person brings a Bible with them to the celebrations, following along with the presider as the biblical text is studied and unpacked. Often the worship services are preceded or followed by small group study of specific biblical books. For these denominations, the Bible is the main source of God's wisdom and guidance. All generations from young to old are taught to read and study the Bible daily, to memorize many of its passages and to attend Sunday school bible study sessions every week.

With regard to studying and understanding the Bible, neither approach is better or more correct. They are simply different approaches that have resulted from the different ways in which Scripture has been used and understood in the various denominations. Each approach has its own advantages and disadvantages.

The Lectionary allows for a more extensive exposure to Scripture while connecting the readings to a particular liturgical season, Sunday, or feast. However, because the readings are taken out of their original context, it is often difficult to know that context. Thus, meaning can be lost or confused. The multiple readings, if not well connected or unified, can be distracting, leaving the listener wondering which passage ought to claim their attention. Most homilists find the number of readings too much to link together in their reflections, often zeroing in on the Gospel as the default focus of their reflections.

On the other hand, direct Bible reading enables one to know the context of the selected passage, often leading to more in-depth understanding of the text. By following in their Bibles, the participants are easily aware of what has gone on before the selected passage, as well as what follows the passage in the biblical text. However, the worship focus is usually on one biblical text, randomly selected by the presider, with little exposure to other texts, and with little or no connection to liturgical seasons or feasts.

Both approaches contain wisdom.

1. How can we ensure that we are exposed to more Scripture, while at the same time delving more in-depth in our study of God's Word?

WHAT IS UNIQUE OR DIFFERENT ABOUT THE WAY CATHOLICS READ AND ARE EXPOSED TO THE BIBLE?

Catholics are exposed to Scripture primarily through the Sunday readings from a book known as the Lectionary. This is a book of selected passages from the Bible set in the context of a particular Sunday in a particular liturgical season, such as Advent, Lent, or Ordinary Time. The Lectionary Scripture readings are divided into a three-year cycle for the Sunday readings Years A, B, and C, and a two-year cycle for the weekday readings Years I and II.

Each of the three Sunday Lectionary years has one of the Synoptic Gospels (Matthew, Mark, and Luke in year A, B, and C, respectively) associated with it. John's Gospel was not given its own liturgical year simply because of its traditional use during the Lenten and Easter seasons.

There are four readings assigned to each Sunday. The first reading is usually taken from the Old Testament, selected to align in some way with the chosen Gospel reading. The first reading is followed by the Responsorial Psalm, a second "reading" made up of selected verses from particular psalms, along with a refrain that captures the theme or responds to the other readings. The third reading is usually from a New Testament letter, which is often read somewhat continuously from week to week. Finally, the Gospel reading is usually taken from the Gospel that is the particular focus of that Lectionary year. This is the usual way in which most Catholics are exposed to the Scriptures.

These readings are taken out of their original context in the Bible and placed in a new context. The selected readings for any given Sunday relate to one another in a manner that is unique to the Lectionary. In essence, the Lectionary relates and connects biblical readings in a manner that does not otherwise exist in the biblical text itself. Placed in close proximity to each other, these readings now have the opportunity to converse with each other in a way that would not have been possible before.

A homilist pays attention to all four readings, preparing a reflection that speaks of this conversation among the readings. Thus, the homily can be a good way of connecting the readings, enabling us to zero in on what this unique combination of God's Word has to say to us this particular Sunday.

Next time you celebrate Sunday liturgy go to http://www.usccb.org/nab. There you will be able to access both the daily and Sunday Lectionary readings. Prepare for Sunday liturgy by reading the Scripture ahead of time. See how this new relationship among the readings addresses and challenges you to be a better Christian here and now.

WHOSE BIBLE IS IT, AND WHAT ROLE DOES EACH FAITH COMMUNITY HAVE IN THE INTERPRETATION OF THE BIBLE?

Our Bible is shared among the three monotheistic religions of the world, namely, Judaism, Christianity, and Islam. Judaism first began the faith reflection on God, the world, and human relationships, resulting in the books of the Bible that Christians refer to as the Old Testament, or the Jewish Scriptures. Catholics highly value the Old Testament because it is the Scripture that Jesus was fed on and lived by. To understand Jesus, one needs to know and understand the Old Testament.

The followers of Jesus produced their own faith reflections on God, the world, and human relationships, which resulted from their experience of the life, mission, and ministry of Jesus. This eventually led to the books of Scripture which we call the New Testament.

Muslims see the Qur'an as a continuation of God's revelations that are in both the Old and New Testaments. The

Qur'an has many similarities and correlations with these revelations, while at the same time offering corrections to what are perceived as errors existing in both Old and New Testaments.

With the Protestant Reformation, Luther translated the Bible from the original languages into German, and in the process did not retain those seven books from the Old Testament that Christians up to that time had come to accept as inspired (and which Catholics still do). So not only do the various Christian denominations have different books in the Old Testament, they also take a different perspective on the interpretation of Scripture.

Since the Reformation, our Protestant brothers and sisters grew suspicious of tradition and thus placed all their focus on Scripture as the only source of authority in living the Christian life. This resulted in a variety of ways to interpret Scripture and apply it to everyday Christian living. For Catholics, both Scripture and tradition flow from Jesus and have their place in guiding us on our faith journey. Other Christians see it differently.

Jews understand their Scriptures, the Christian Old Testament, as articulating for them their covenant relationship with God. This leads the Jewish community to interpret the Scriptures through the lens of their faith experience. Muslims use the Qur'an as revelations that correlate with the Old and New Testament, while at the same time correcting and modifying what they see as errors in both. Other Christians interpret and understand Scripture from their particular faith expression and reality, emphasizing those things that will help them in living out their Christian faith lives. Catholics do the same thing as other Christians in interpreting the Bible. But they add elements that are often minimized or eliminated in other Christian denominations. Catholics see tradition as another font of revelation while accepting the teaching office of the church as guiding them to the proper interpretation of Scripture.

It is obvious that the same book for Jews and Christians is used differently and interpreted differently. The Qur'an is another entity closely related to the Jewish and Christian Scriptures and yet understood by them as going beyond both Jewish and Christian Scripture in correctness and totality of revelation. Ultimately, the same Scriptures belong to more than one faith community. It is the responsibility of each faith community to interpret the Scriptures for their community, while at the same time respecting the other's interpretation, even if it might disagree. Only in this manner can we maintained unity in our belief in one God, and at the same time respect our differences and the richness of our diversity.

1. How do you relate to someone who interprets or understands a particular Scripture passage differently from you?
2. How can this experience become an occasion for mutual dialogue, understanding, and respect for the varied richness of our different traditions?

How are Catholic Bibles different from Protestant Bibles?

Today, all reputable Bibles are translations from the original Hebrew or Greek. In that sense, there is little difference between them when it comes to the actual text being translated from the original languages. There might be some disagreements among scholars as to the arrangement of some passages, but there is general agreement about the overall translation.

There are several ways, however, that Protestant and Catholic Bibles differ. One way concerns the study notes, essays, footnotes, and introductions to the biblical books. These usually reflect the beliefs and experience of the denomination that sponsored or oversaw the translation. A Baptist- or Catholic-sponsored translation will display that denomination's bent in the way it understands or interprets the texts.

Another key difference has to do with the number of books included in their Bible, as well as the way those books are arranged. This difference impacts only the Old Testament. In general, there are seven books and some other additions that Catholics accept as having been inspired by God that both Protestants and Jews do not accept. (See the tables on pages 73–75.)

WHY AND HOW DOES THE OLD TESTAMENT IN CATHOLIC BIBLES DIFFER FROM JEWISH SCRIPTURES AND PROTESTANT BIBLES?

The story begins with Jewish Scripture itself. By the third century BCE, Greek was the international language of commerce, politics, education, and culture. About 250 BCE, a Greek translation of Scripture was commissioned by Jews who lived outside of Palestine and who could not read or understand Hebrew. This translation, known as the Septuagint, was used on a regular basis by Jews outside of Palestine. As more biblical books written in Greek were added to this translation, the Septuagint expanded, and the books were arranged differently from the Hebrew Scriptures.

When the followers of Jesus were carrying on his mission to the people outside of Israel, they used the Septuagint translation since it was in a language more of them understood. This translation became the one that Christians eventually included in their Bibles when they began to select the definitive inspired list of books. The Jews were deciding on a definitive list at the same time. The Jews decided to include only those books originally written in Hebrew rather than Greek. Thus, they rejected the additions that had been made to the Septuagint. The Christians accepted those additions, calling them deutero-canonical, or "second canon."

In 1521, when Martin Luther translated the Old Testament from the original languages into German, he noticed the differences between the number of books in the Jewish Scriptures and those in the Christian Bibles. Luther felt that the Jewish Scriptures were more authentic in their inspiration than the ones currently used by the Christians. So in his translation, he maintained the order of books in the Christian Old Testament but removed the books that were not included in the Jewish Scriptures.

To this day, Protestant translations of the Bible will not include those books, which they call the Apocrypha. However, they will print editions of the Bible that include the Apocrypha, thus making their translation available for use by Catholics as well.

The tables below specify the arrangement as well as the list of books that are included in Jewish Scripture and in Protestant and Catholic Bibles. Books in italics are found only in Catholic Bibles.

Jewish Canon	Protestant Canon	Roman Catholic Canon
Tanak	Old Testament	Old Testament
1. Torah (Torah) Genesis Exodus Leviticus Numbers Deuteronomy	1. Pentateuch Genesis Exodus Leviticus Numbers Deuteronomy	1. Pentateuch Genesis Exodus Leviticus Numbers Deuteronomy
2. Prophets (Nevi'im) Former Prophets Joshua Judges	2. Historical Books Joshua Judges Ruth	2. Historical Books Joshua Judges Ruth

Continued next page

Jewish Canon	Protestant Canon	Roman Catholic Canon
Tanak	**Old Testament**	**Old Testament**
Samuel	1 and 2 Samuel	1 and 2 Samuel
Kings	1 and 2 Kings	1 and 2 Kings
Four Books of	1 and 2 Chronicles	1 and 2 Chronicles
Latter Prophets	Ezra	Ezra
Isaiah	Nehemiah	Nehemiah
Jeremiah	Esther	*Tobit*
Ezekiel		*Judith*
The Twelve (one		Esther *(plus additions)*
book)		1 and 2 Maccabees
Hosea	**3. Wisdom**	
Joel	Job	**3. Wisdom**
Amos	Psalms	Job
Obadiah	Proverbs	Psalms
Jonah	Ecclesiastes	Proverbs
Micah	Song of Songs	Ecclesiastes
Nahum		Song of Songs
Habakkuk	**4. Prophets**	*Wisdom of Solomon*
Zephaniah	Isaiah	*Ecclesiasticus (or*
Haggai	Jeremiah	*Sirach)*
Zechariah	Lamentations	
Malachi	Ezekiel	**4. Prophets**
	Daniel	Isaiah
3. Writings (Kethuvim)	Hosea	Jeremiah
Psalms	Joel	Lamentations
Job	Amos	*Baruch*
Proverbs	Obadiah	*Letter of Jeremiah*
Ruth	Jonah	Ezekiel
Song of Songs	Micah	Daniel *(plus the Prayer*
Ecclesiastes	Nahum	*of Azariah, Song of*
Lamentations	Habakkuk	*the Three Young Men,*
Esther	Zephaniah	*Susanna, Bel and the*

Continued next page

Continued

Jewish Canon	Protestant Canon	Roman Catholic Canon
Tanak	**Old Testament**	**Old Testament**
Daniel Ezra-Nehemiah Chronicles	Haggai Zechariah Malachi	*Dragon)* Hosea Joel Amos Obadiah Jonah Micah Nahum Habakkuk Zephaniah Haggai Zechariah Malachi

7

Techniques for Sharing the Scriptures with Others

WHAT IS BIBLE STUDY AND HOW CAN ONE DO SUCH STUDY EFFECTIVELY?

Bible study addresses the basic question, "What does the text mean?" In order to understand the text properly, more than simply reading the Scripture is necessary. Bible study enables the participants to know the author and the community that put this text together. It analyzes the date and the sources of this particular book, along with the literary style and the unique arrangement that the author used to get God's Word across. Bible study focuses on what the text said and meant at the time that it was written. What message was the text trying to communicate to the community for whom it was intended? What were the needs and concerns of that community, which this text was choosing to address?

In order to do this effectively, people doing Bible study can access a variety of study aids that assist them in effectively unpacking the text. Necessary study aids include dictionaries of the Bible, along with atlases. Both provide the necessary historical and visual backdrop needed to make sense of the culture, the history, and the geography of places mentioned in the text. A concordance is helpful to find other passages that contain the same word or phrase. For example, a concordance will list all the passages in the Bible that have the word *love* or *widow* or whatever word you might be exploring.

Finally, a necessary resource for Bible study is a commentary, which offers a variety of information on the biblical text. It analyzes the language of the text, often giving nuances of the original that might be missing in the current translation we are reading. It then situates each part of the text within the framework of the whole book, as well as makes any connections that this text might have to other biblical books. Finally, it attempts to analyze what the text meant to the community that produced it, along with what the text may mean to us as we apply it to our day and age. A commentary consistently offers much that will enable readers to understand a text more clearly and with greater insight.

To do Bible study effectively, these are some necessary resources. The process may appear intimidating, but the more familiar one becomes with these resources, the more one will begin to see the text with new depth, enriching it and bringing it to life.

WHAT IS DEVOTIONAL OR SPIRITUAL READING OF THE BIBLE?

There is a great deal of confusion regarding the distinctions between Bible study and devotional or spiritual reading of the Bible. Many people feel inadequate when it comes to reading the Bible, simply because they feel that they do not have enough background to properly read, understand, or interpret the biblical text.

One purpose of reading Scripture is Bible study, analyzing the text to ascertain how it spoke to the community who put it together, addressing the question, "What does the text mean?" People sometimes feel overwhelmed by Bible study and intimidated by all that is involved in properly studying the Bible.

Devotional or spiritual reading of the Bible approaches the text to learn what God might be saying to me in my life here and now, hopefully learning from its wisdom so that I can draw closer to God. This type of Bible reading explores the text in an attempt to answer the question, "What does the text mean to me?" Both types of reading are essential to understand the Scripture text fully. Here we will focus on the spiritual reading of the text.

Spiritual or devotional reading of the Bible can be an excellent way to familiarize oneself with the text and to milk it for its spiritual wisdom and insights. The Christian tradition has called this exercise *Lectio divina*, the divine or spiritual reading of the text. This approach does not dwell so much on the historical aspects of the text or its original audience and context. Rather, *lectio divina* focuses on delving into the text with an open heart and mind, attuning ourselves to what God might want to highlight for us as we reflect on the text and apply it to our lives. This is an excellent method for private devotion or for faith sharing in small groups, learning from sharing with others, and being enriched by the reflections that others have on the reading at hand.

Lectio divina is a simple process that begins with attuning ourselves to the presence of God. Calling upon the Spirit, we ask for openness of hearts and minds that we may be receptive to how God speaks to us in and through the Scripture text, as well as in and through the reflections of others who are reflecting on the same text. The reflection focuses on some simple questions that guide us in gleaning spiritual wisdom and applications from the text. The first step begins with reading the text aloud, silently selecting a word or phrase that attracts or speaks to you. Dwelling on the word or phrase for a period of time helps us to move to the next step.

In the second step, ask yourself how and where the content of this reading touches your life today. What connections are you making between the words that attract you in the reading and your everyday life? Taking time to share that with the group will lead to more connections as we learn from others what has attracted them and what connections they are making with their lives.

The last step in the *lectio divina* process involves the "So what?" question. In light of my reflection, what action does this reading call me to? What does God want me to do in response to the insights, wisdom, and connections I have been led to in my reflection on the reading? This action step can be as simple as doing one thing this week that will help me be a better friend or spouse. Or it can call me to a long-range plan of action, moving me to some significant new direction in my life, more in tune with God's plans rather than mine.

To summarize, *lectio divina* consists of a three-step process of reflection on any particular biblical text:

1. Pick a word or phrase that attracts you.
2. How and where does the content of this reading touch your life today?
3. I believe that God wants me to _____ over this coming week (month, year, lifetime).

Select one of the Sunday Eucharist readings for personal and group reflection before celebrating the Sunday liturgy. Using the *lectio divina* method will help unpack that reading, helping you to make life connections with that reading. As you celebrate the liturgy, your reflection on that reading will help you be more attuned to its message for your life. A well-prepared homily will help you make more connections.

This week, use the *lectio divina* process on one of the readings for the coming Sunday and make a note of the life connections you are making. How is this reflection on the biblical text drawing you closer to God and others?

WHAT ARE THE FOUR QUESTIONS THAT HELP FURTHER OUR UNDERSTANDING OF THE MESSAGE AND STRUCTURE OF ANY BIBLE PASSAGE OR BOOK?

In order to interpret a biblical book effectively, certain aspects of that text must be explored. One method that helps move toward effective interpretation involves asking several questions of the text, milking it for as much information as possible, to get at the heart and intention of the original author and community who composed it.

When a text is read, asking the questions listed below greatly helps in getting at the fullness of the text's message. Consistently asking these questions will also help in learning from the text (*exegesis*) rather than imposing our views on the text (*eisegesis*).

The questions are:

1. What is the situation or context that forms the backdrop to this text?
2. What are the individual or community needs that surface out of this context?
3. What is the message that the community wanted to communicate to those experiencing this context and these needs?
4. How did the community choose to communicate that message? What shape or form did the community give to the meaning and wisdom it had distilled from its experience?

The first question affirms the reality that the text was written at a particular, historical time and place. The language, customs, cultural, and social contexts are all important factors needing exploration, so that misunderstanding and misreading does not occur.

Once this context has been determined, an examination of the needs that exist in that community can be explored. The needs will shape what must be addressed in light of the God of reality and experience. Once these needs are identified, one begins to understand the message that the author and the community want to communicate. This message reflects the insight and reflections, the meaning and significance that God has for this community in light of its context and needs.

Finally, the last question examines the methods and means used to communicate the message effectively and creatively to capture the attention and imagination of that community, as well as others reading the text. Things like sources and language used, literary styles, stories or parables included, and other techniques or literary devices speak to the audience's context and needs.

HOW CAN THE "FOCUSED CONVERSATION" METHOD BE USED TO REFLECT ON THE BIBLICAL TEXT?

Besides *lectio divina*, another method that can be used to help in connecting the biblical text to everyday life is a process known as a "focused conversation." Focused conversations help greatly in getting at the heart of the text and applying it to everyday life, making connections that hopefully will help each of us draw closer to God.

A focused conversation begins by zeroing in on a text that we wish to explore for the sake of spiritual and devotional reading and reflecting. This method can be used for individual reflection or in a group. The process described below is adapted to a group context (See Laura J. Spencer's *Winning through Participation*). It describes a series of steps and questions that are asked as one walks through the process. The first question asks for an objective response, the second requires a feelings/emotions response, the third challenges with an interpretive response, while the last demands an action response or a "What does this mean for me?" response, leading to some future resolve or plan of action.

Before beginning, let us look at the overall directions to the process.

Overall Directions

1. Select the biblical passage on which the group wishes to reflect. It would be good to have a copy of the text for each participant so that they can mark up the text, adding their reflections and insights as they go along.
2. Before reading the passage, share with the group the first question you will ask them. (See below.)
3. Read the Scripture once. Pause for a while and then read it again.
4. Ask the first question. Several questions are asked at each step. They essentially use different words aiming

to tap into the different ways that people might react to the text.

5. Responses to the first question should be brief. Ask only for a short answer (one word or a phrase of two or three words). Ask each person to respond, moving around the group from one person to the next. No comments or questions are permitted at this time.

6. Ask the second question and invite anyone to respond.

7. Do the same with questions three and four allowing as many responses as time allows.

8. Follow-up questions and open discussion can occur at any time from the second question onward.

9. The facilitator of the focused conversation needs to be attuned to the time set aside for sharing, as well as when it is time to move on to the next question.

10. All four questions need to be explored for the reflection to move to implications and finally action.

The four areas to be explored and the possible questions that one can ask are listed below. Do not hesitate to make up your own wording to the questions, as long as you maintain the intent of the area to be explored.

1. Objective: Just the facts, sensory data

What is one word or phrase in this passage that you heard? What is a one-word image that this Scripture brings to your mind? Who is one character named in this reading? And so on.

2. Reflective: Emotions, feelings, associations

What excited you about what you heard? What one thing surprised you about this passage? What caught your attention? What challenged you in this passage? What concerns or questions surfaced for you as you heard this passage? And so on.

3. Interpretive: Values, meaning, purpose

What does this passage mean for those of us who live in this community? What is the most valuable part of the reading for you? What would we be like if we lived as this passage calls us to live? And so on.

4. Decisional: Future resolves, future action, and/or closure, the next step

What would you like this community/parish/class to be aware of because of this reading? What would be your theme if you had to teach about the message and insights of this passage? What are you left wondering about at the end of this Scripture? What will you do differently as a result of reflecting on this reading? And so on.

These questions, when used consistently with each Bible book or passage, will greatly enhance our understanding of and appreciation for the truth of the message that God wants to communicate. This understanding offers help in our faith journey toward ultimate union with God.

What are multiple intelligences, and how can I use them to help me reflect on biblical passages in a variety of creative ways?

Multiple intelligences recognize that people process information and learn in a variety of ways. Each individual has a dominant intelligence type that leads to a preferred way of learning. The learning process too often has focused on the most often-used intelligence styles.

If a teacher, a catechist, a homilist, or any speaker wants to attract, influence, and inspire others, then being attuned to the various ways in which people learn is essential. Presentations that involve most or all of these intelligences will engage most of the people in the group, thus making for more effective and pervasive learning and reflection by the whole group.

Below is a description of multiple intelligences adapted from *Awakening the Genius in Every Child* by Thomas Armstrong. These multiple intelligences are present in adults as well as children.

- **Linguistic**: How can I use the spoken or written word?
- **Intrapersonal**: How can I evoke personal feelings or memories or give participants choices?
- **Interpersonal**: How can I engage participants in peer sharing, cooperative learning, or large group simulation?

- **Naturalist**: How can I incorporate living things or systems?
- **Bodily-Kinesthetic**: How can I involve the whole body or use hands-on experience?
- **Musical**: How can I bring in music or environmental sounds, or set key points in a rhythmic or melodic framework?
- **Spatial**: How can I use visual aids, visualization, color, art, or metaphor?
- **Logical-Mathematical**: How can I bring in numbers, calculations, logic, classifications, or critical thinking skills?

This awareness of multiple intelligences is applied to the spiritual reading and reflection on a biblical text. A process is outlined for how to engage people with the biblical text so that all of the various ways of learning and reflecting are encouraged. This method can be put to good use in any group or class session.

Overall directions for using multiple intelligences

1. Write the various words and descriptions for multiple intelligences on newsprint or posters and hang them around the room.
2. Invite participants to choose and go stand by one of the eight areas that they are attracted to in terms of learning and processing information.

3. Present a phrase, theme, parable, or event from Scripture. The Sunday readings could be a rich source for these passages.
4. Have each group take the phrase, theme, parable, or Scripture event and illustrate it, using the intelligence style they have chosen to explore.
5. Have each group discuss how they would teach this concept, phrase, theme, parable, or Scripture event using this particular style.
6. Invite each group to share their response with the large group.
7. The response can be done reflectively as prayer, as a discussion, or as both.
8. End by evaluating, possibly using a focused conversation method discussed previously.

ARE THERE OTHER CREATIVE WAYS TO REFLECT ON THE SCRIPTURES AND APPLY THEM TO EVERYDAY LIFE?

Besides the various methods described previously, there are some other creative ways of unpacking the Scriptures and articulating what they mean in an individual's life, here and now. These approaches can be used to unpack and unravel the Scriptures, either individually or in a group.

Scripture and the News/Newspaper

1. Take the Scriptures for the coming Sunday.

2. Zero in on some key headline stories in the newspaper, radio, TV, or Internet news.
3. Proclaim the Scriptures aloud.
4. Correlate the Scriptures with the news items, discussing what light one might possibly shine on the other.
5. In prayerful reflection discuss how the events in the news relate to the message or themes of the Scripture being proclaimed.
6. A focused conversation method (see previous pages) or some other discussion process can be used.
7. End with prayers praising or thanking God or asking God for whatever you feel is needed in your life and in the world.

Take a Stand: Phrases from Scripture

1. Select a passage from Scripture from the coming Sunday or one that you would like to reflect on individually or with a group.
2. Before proclaiming the Scripture passage, select significant phrases from the passage and write them on newsprint or poster board.
3. Hang them around the room in various locations separate from each other.
4. Proclaim the Scripture passage aloud.
5. After proclaiming the passage, give each person time to connect with the various phrases you have selected and pasted around the room.

6. Ask each person to go and stand by the Scripture phrase that draws them. It may challenge, comfort, upset, or cause that individual to question, or more. Hopefully more than one person will select and stand by each phrase.
7. Have people share with others who have chosen the same phrase and reflect on why they chose this phrase.
8. Some people might choose to dialogue with others who have chosen a different phrase, sharing why they have chosen one phrase over the other.
9. Think of creative variations that could jump off from this process. For example, one variation could be to have participants choose a phrase which says something about what they believe and have them make a sign that they might carry at a demonstration or a poster that they might use to proclaim their thoughts to others.

"Playing" in the Scriptures

1. Choose a character from a biblical story or passage and "get inside" the person.
   - What is he or she thinking, feeling, wondering?
   - How are they connecting to what is happening?
   - What are they seeing, hearing, smelling, touching, tasting?
   - What connections are they making about everyday life?

2. Share your insights and reflections with the group by speaking as if you were that character, using the first person, bringing that character to life for your group.
3. A variation of this exercise could be to put a *new* character into the story and go through the same process.
4. Another variation could be to place yourself into the story as either an observer or a participant. Who would you be and what would you be doing? Share your improvisation with the group.

Symbols and Scripture

1. Select a Scripture passage from the coming Sunday readings or from a biblical passage that you would like to unpack for reflection.
2. Gather some symbols either mentioned in the Scripture passage or associated with the story.
3. Place the gathered symbols in the midst of the group. Ask the group to reflect individually on the items they see—how they are used, what symbolism each carries, what meaning it has for the individual.
4. After some quiet time, ask each person to share what thoughts or feelings came to them while reflecting on the symbols.
5. Then read the Scripture, have the participants seek connections, and reflect on those connections in relationship to their everyday life.
6. Close with prayers of praise, thanksgiving, or petition to our loving God.

The Cinquain and Scripture

1. Select a Scripture passage from the coming Sunday readings or from a biblical passage that you would like to unpack for reflection.
2. Ask group participants to zero in on the passage by using the following literary format, ordinarily known as a cinquain (sin-kwane), which is a five-line poetry stanza. For each line, use the structure below.

First line: one noun

Second line: two adjectives

Third line: three "ing" words

Fourth line: one phrase (not necessarily from Scripture)

Fifth line: one synonym for the noun

3. Below is a cinquain based on John 10:1–28 about Jesus as the Good Shepherd.

Jesus
Alert, Protective
Guiding, Encouraging, Urging
"I know mine and mine know me"
Shepherd

OTHER BOOKS IN THIS SERIES

Connecting with Parents
Mary Twomey Spollen

Teaching the Faith
Kim Duty

Praying with Young People
Maureen Gallagher

Planning Your Teaching Year
Monica A. Hughes

Connecting with Parents
A Catechist's Guide to Involving Parents in
Their Child's Religious Formation
Mary Twomey Spollen
This book is a practical guide for volunteer catechists
who want to include parents in the ongoing
catechesis of their children.
978-0-8091-4469-3

Praying with Young People
Tips for Catechists
Maureen Gallagher
A Seasoned catechetical director offers Scripture-based prayer suggestions for young people under the catechist's care.
978-0-8091-4401-3

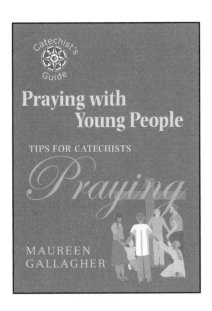

Teaching the Faith
A Catechist's Guide to Classroom Management
Kim Duty

A reader-friendly book that provides useful help,
information, ideas, advice, and motivation
for every beginning catechist.

978-0-8091-4400-6

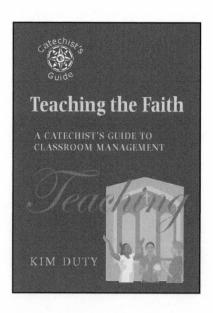

Planning Your Teaching Year
A Catechist's Guide to
Developing Effective Goals
Monica A. Hughes

Designed to assist both new and existing catechists
in the process of effective organization and
planning for their current year of service
as a catechist or teacher of religion.

978-0-8091-4569-0

101 Questions & Answers on the Bible

Raymond E. Brown

A noted biblical scholar's concise responses to
a wide range of the questions most frequently
posed to him about the Bible.

0-8091-4251-1

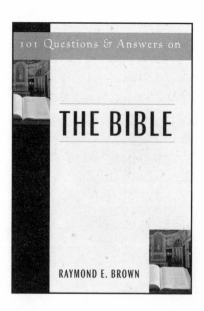

Reading the Old Testament: An Introduction

Lawrence Boadt, CSP

"The most up-to-date, clearly written, carefully arranged, and comprehensive general introduction to the Old Testament." ——The Bible Today

Can be used as a companion text to the Paulist Bible Study Program.

0-8091-2631-1

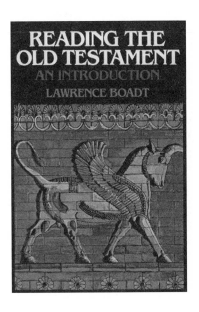

Reading the New Testament: An Introduction, Second Edition

Pheme Perkins

Outlines of every book in the New Testament; information from archaeology and social history that has come to light in the past decade; new maps and illustrative material, and revised bibliography.

0-8091-2939-6

A Walk Through the New Testament

An Introduction for Catholics

Margaret Nutting Ralph

A companion volume for adult Catholics as they read the New Testament, helping them apply the Catholic approach to Scripture.

978-0-8091-4582-9

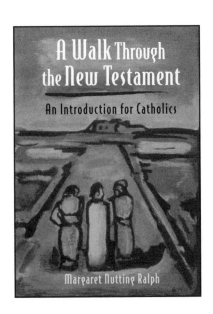

The Catholic Prayer Bible
(NRSV)
Lectio Divina Edition

An ideal Bible for anyone who desires to reflect on the individual stories and chapters of just one, or even all, of the biblical books, while being led to prayer though meditation on that biblical passage.

978-0-8091-4663-5 Paperback
978-0-8091-0587-8 Hardcover

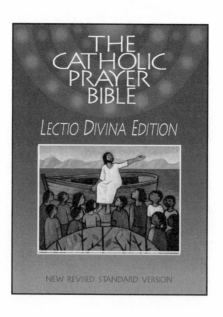

Understanding the Bible
(Revised & Expanded Edition)
A Basic Introduction to Biblical Interpretation
George T. Montague
A popular overview, newly revised and expanded, of
the ways scripture has been interpreted from biblical
times to the present, with an evaluation of ancient
and contemporary methods.
978-0-8091-4344-3

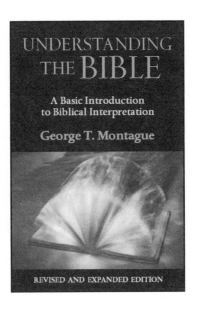

Echoing the Word
An Introductory Catechist Formation Process
Gretchen Hailer

An introduction and interactive process for
parish-based catechist formation. This process is an
opportunity for everyone involved in catechetical
ministry to explore the importance of faith
formation for adults, youth, and children,
supported by church teaching and documents.

978-0-8091-4563-8